Happy Birthday, Vict —
this is the next
best thing to a ticket there!
x x x
Nina & Damn Sam

Oct. - 1999

To my Grandmother, with special thanks to Noemi and my mother. — *Stefano*

To Nooney, Orietta, and Mom, who taught me to travel, took me in, and welcomed me home. — *Kelley*

COVER
Hidden behind a village wall, the estate of Montelopio is a retreat for golfers who play at nearby Castelfalfa.

FOLLOWING PAGE
Eighteenth-century map of Italy carved into a stone tabletop.

First published in the United States of America in 1999 by
UNIVERSE PUBLISHING
A Division of Rizzoli International Publications, Inc.
300 Park Avenue South
New York, NY 10010

Distributed in the U.S. trade by St. Martin's Press, New York
Distributed in Canada by McClelland and Stewart

99 00 01 / 10 9 8 7 6 5 4 3 2 1

Printed in Italy

Design by Amelia Costigan

ITALIAN COUNTRY HIDEAWAYS

Vacationing in Tuscany's and Umbria's Private Villas, Castles, and Estates

Photography by Stefano Hunyady

Text by Kelley F. Hurst

UNIVERSE

Val di Paro
Duche de Modene
Modene
Sasseu
Spilanbergo
C. Franco
Castel
Bologne
Faenza
Rauene
Apenin
Parma
Preda
Guia
Bolognese
Imola
Romagne
Cas. Bolognese
Forli
Cesena
Pontremoli
Sestola
Frignano
Casio
Rimini
Bertenore
Carrara
S. Marin
Castiglion
del Sole
Fiuizano
Minochiano
Castiglia
Sarsina
Castiglianno
Fiorenzola
Barga
Spedale
Barberin
Florentin
S. Leo
Apennin
Lerici
Sarezano
Estat de
Camaldoli
Scarparia
Urbino
Norgno
Pistoia
Prato
Fiesoli
Valombrosa
Borgo S. Sepolcro
Piersanta
De Lucques
Pescia
M. Pogio
Florence
Viareggio
S. Casano
Francho
Arezo
Lucques
Grand Duche
Empoli
a Era
Panzano
Civitella
Castiglione
Citta di Castelo
Cassine
Pogibonsi
Arne
Pisa
M. Foscoli
M. S. Maria
Cortone
Perugia
Volterra
Colle
Stagia
Liuorne
De Toscane
Siene
Gorgona
Vada
Sienois
Bonconuento
M. Pulciano
C. della Pieve
Le Pomerance
M. Rufoli
Pienza
Mont Alcino
Alcino
Chiusi
Orvieto
Todi
Campiglia
Massa
S. Quirico
Radicofani
M. Nero
Capraia
Ciuitela
M. Pescali
Scarlino
Acqua pendente
Bolsena
Sforzasca
Viterbo
Montealto
Groseto
Soana
P. Feraio
Piombino
M. Iano
M. Marano
Valenta
S. Fiorenzo
Troia I.
P. Longon
Talamon
Duche
Farnese
Fiascone
de Castro
Toscanela
Nebbio
P. S. Stefano
Orbitele
Ansedonia
M. Alto
Patrimoine
Elbe I.
la Bastie
Formiche
Corneto
Marcana
Formiche
Corse
P. Ercole
Monte Cristo
Giglio
Monte Argentaro
Ciuita Vechia
Aleria
Corse
Gianuti
Porto S.
Corsina

TABLE OF CONTENTS

FOREWORD

IMAGINE YOURSELF SIPPING ONE OF ITALY'S FINEST VINTAGES in a seventeenth-century *cantina* (wine cellar) with the winemaker; or sitting *en famille* in a country villa's fresco-adorned dining room, eating hearty Italian country fare of fresh or cured meats, locally made Pecorino cheese, homemade pasta tossed with a just-picked tomato and basil sauce, and vegetables picked from the garden, drizzled with olive oil; or imagine being nudged out of bed by the sun to gaze out your tower bedroom window over the peaceful, rolling hills of the Volterrana, framing the towers of San Gimignano a few hilltops away.

These images may fill an afternoon in a favorite chair or serve as an inspiration for your next trip to the land of Dante and St. Francis of Assisi. In either case, we offer you a private tour of many of our favorite estates in this intriguing landscape of the ancient Etruscans. We ask only that you exchange, if momentarily, the excitement of Italy's magnificent cities for the enchantment of her green heart.

Agriturismo, the renting of a villa or an apartment in a *castello* (castle), fortress, or a *podere* (farmhouse) on a *tenuta* (estate) or *fattoria* (farm) for an Italian country vacation, offers a chance to savor living among the cypress-lined paths and undulating, vineyard-covered hills of Chianti or in a mountainside retreat near the sea. The manner of living on these estates has been developed over the centuries by a synergy of diverse elements: noble families; a system of agriculture to support the estate (during feudal times, the *mezzadria,* or tenant farming, method); the legends, mythology, and history passed down through the centuries; the artisans; wine and olive oil; fresh local foods; the battles from medieval city-state sieges to world wars; and the generations of people who have tended these bountiful acres.

This book illuminates thirty estates among the hundreds, chosen after careful research, personal visits, and the ability to meet the following criteria. First, the estate's primary business must be the production of wine, olive oil, cheese, the raising of horses, or some other economy that connects it inextricably to the land. This commitment to the countryside is tangibly reflected in the owner's love of his wine or the unwavering guarantee that his *frantoio*'s (olive oil mill) method of pressing the olives produces the best oil. Second, each estate must provide accommodations, and typically, is not well known to the majority of travelers. The third, and most subjective criteria, is that each estate must possess a special intangible quality, something that truly sets it apart: a notable history, unforgettable food, spectacular views, or some other outstanding feature so compelling that it merits particular attention.

Each one of these estates contributes individually to the overall character of Tuscany and Umbria; and with the help of the following imagery and information, this book will guide you to the destination within this untamed yet highly civilized region of Italy that most captures your imagination. We hope to leave you enchanted, enamored of this pristine countryside and, quite possibly, reaching for your passport.

THE HILLS OF FLORENCE

WIELDING A MAGICAL MAGNETISM FOR ART AND WINE LOVERS, THE CITY OF FLORENCE IS A HAVEN OF CULTURAL DELIGHTS AND HER SURROUNDING HILLS PROVE NO LESS ENCHANTING. THESE HILLS, which flank the city in a northern half moon, west to east from Pistoia to Rufina, encompass two wine-making regions coveted for exceptional, well-aging wines and are dotted with an abundance of resplendent villas and castles. The first renowned DOCG wine area is the Chianti Rufina, reached from Florence by traveling upstream along the Arno River and eastward to Sieci, then north into the Sieve River valley. Wine experts describe the Chianti Rufina as the most likely wine among the Chianti cousins (other than Chianti Classico) to be long-lived and of excellent quality. Chianti Rufina counts among its finest producers the Frescobaldi family and the estates at Selvapiana and Bossi. The estate of Colognole is showing great promise as it reestablishes its vines. Like Chianti Rufina, the region of Carmignano, west of Florence, is home to a highly valued wine of limited production. Clarke and Spurrier, noted wine writers *(Fine Wine Guide,* 1998), indicate that the riserva version of Carmignano, made only in the best years, "favours elegance over power." This tiny DOCG wine area is well-represented by producers Artimino, Il Poggiolo, Ambra, Bacchereto, and Ugo Contini Bonacossi's Capezzana estate. This natural haven in the cool hills has been appreciated for centuries; wealthy families built extensive homes as a respite from the bustling city. The Medici acquired Il Trebbio for hunting, and Cafaggiolo as a summer home; Careggi near Sesto Fiorentino became a favorite retreat, and now houses a notable nineteenth-century English garden. Castello also has extensive gardens, replete with mid-sixteenth-century water works, and Poggio a Caiano near Capezzana is immediately recognizable by its portico designed by Sangallo, with an unusual blue-and-white enamel frieze.

VIEWS OF FLORENCE *In the hills surrounding Florence are the architectural monuments to her first family, the Medici, who transformed many military outposts into breathtaking country residences. Il Trebbio, pictured here (opposite), was their favorite hunting lodge.* PAGE 8–9 *Rows of grape vines blanket the hills outside of Florence.*

AZIENDA AGRICOLA COLOGNOLE

The Colognole estate was purchased by the grandmother of Gabriella Spalletti Trivelli in 1865; today, Gabriella and her sons, Mario and Cesare Coda, fulfill the family's mission of recreating the old way of estate living by carefully restoring and preserving its nearly 2,000 acres. As Mario Coda states, "We want to keep the whole estate alive." They achieve this ideal through responsibly balancing and personally overseeing all of the estate's endeavors, including the Chianti Rufina DOCG area vineyards, olive groves, forestry, hunting, the offices and wine bottling in the villa, the houses, the restaurant at the top of the mountain, and agritourism.

The estate's property lies between the Sieve River and the top of a mountain named Montegiovi. This landscape lends itself well to scenic walks that traverse the woods and encircle the mountain. In the late 1200s, the noted sculptor, painter, and architect Giotto spent his formative years as an artist at the Colognole estate and may have been inspired by his walks here. There are circular markers for "Giotto's path," as this brilliant artist is remembered not only for his campanile in Florence, but also, possibly through legend, for drawing perfect circles. Gabriella Spalletti's family strives to maintain the beauty and balance of the estate so that more than seven hundred years after Giotto, today's generations may appreciate Colognole's pristine beauty, invisibly managed by the human hand.

VIEWS OF COLOGNOLE *(opposite) The entry to the seventeenth-century villa "La Fattoria," one of the houses available for rent.* PAGE 12, CLOCKWISE, FROM TOP LEFT *Colognole's grape harvest; exterior view of "La Fattoria."; the center of the estate's business concerns, Villa Colognole; located within the Chianti Rufina DOCG area, Azienda Agricola Colognole began to produce red and white wine again in 1990, after a long hiatus.* PAGE 13 *Two generations of leadership: Gabriella Spalletti and Mario Coda, one of her two sons who manage the estate.*

COLOGNOLE
BIANCO DEI COLLI
1996
VINO DA TAVOLA
GABRIELLA SPALLETTI
PROPRIETARIA - VITICOLTORE

TENUTA DI BOSSI

In 1592, the Gondi family decided to purchase Tenuta di Bossi as a country home; they have owned the farm ever since. The fifteenth-century villa was modified with a French influence in the nineteenth century, which added a floor and altered the facade. The name "Bossi" means "boxwood"—a shrub normally associated with formal Italianate gardens. The villa and estate, though approached through a semiformal garden, are tucked into the hills of Chianti Rufina and surrounded by forests and wild Avlignese horses. Somehow, on Bossi's nearly 800 acres, the Gondi family manages to balance the wildness of the woods with the regimen of grapevine and olive tree cultivation. The Gondi family has been practicing viniculture here for the last two hundred years, and, currently, Tenuta di Bossi produces six wines, a *vin santo,* and a *grappa.* The estate's olive oil dates back even further; its own *orci,* terra cotta olive oil storage pots, date to the 1700s.

VIEWS OF BOSSI
(opposite) The Gondi family, whose name originated in the Mugello in the thirteenth century, is known for its winemaking. Pictured here is the dessert wine, called vin santo, *stored in the wine cellar. (below) Villa Bossi, which is home to the owners and is the business center.* FOLLOWING PAGES *Grapes drying on bamboo mats in the* vin santaia. Vin santo *is made by waiting several months to press the grapes after they are picked, thus allowing most of their water to evaporate. Once the grapes are pressed, the wine is then aged in barrels for several years.*

CASTELLO IL TREBBIO

"So was I led by a dazzling gleam of crystal hexagons
To plains immaculate in enchanted lands
Where a boundless surface for time immortal
Awaits an imprint of the perfect verse. . . ." [1]

Trebbio castle, which lies just above its cousin Cafaggiolo, was part of the noble Medici family holdings from the fifteenth to the mid-seventeenth centuries. Generations of Medici bankers, statesmen, and supporters of the arts, so closely aligned with the history of Florence, come from this area called the Mugello, a plain in the shadow of the main range of the Apennine Mountains. The Medicis' migration to Florence around 1200 from the Mugello region did not diminish their attachment to their ancestral homeland, which is reflected in their efforts to preserve and restore these two *castelli.*

The tower of the Trebbio castle is over a thousand years old; the outer walls of the castle were built in 1066. Under the guidance of Cosimo de' Medici (also known as Cosimo the Elder), the castle was fortified and roofed in 1427 by the noted Florentine architect, sculptor, and engraver of gems, Bartolommeo di Gherardo di Michelozzo Michelozzi. It was also during the fifteenth century that the dramatic pergola was created in the garden.

The landmark castle and garden stand as testaments to the integrity of Medieval construction, the strength of Renaissance renovation, and the commitment of its owners, from the ancient Medici to the present-day Scaretti.

[1] Lorenzo Scaretti, inspired to poetry by the snow blanketing the country surrounding Trebbio Castle. Excerpted from "Winter; One Sunday Morning" from his collection, *The Four Seasons in Italy.*

VIEWS OF TREBBIO

PREVIOUS PAGE *The castle of Trebbio, which produces olive oil and raises Haflinger ponies, is closely identified with the Renaissance Medici family.* THIS PAGE *(right) A plaque commemorating former resident Amerigo Vespucci, credited with the discovery of America. (below) The stunning pergola within the garden of Il Trebbio.* FOLLOWING PAGE *A view into the castle's courtyard.*

FATTORIA DI MAIANO

Maiano's estate bridges two distinct worlds. A spectacular view of the center of Florence just beyond the villa's gardens reveals the proximity of the great city's landmarks—a mere twenty-minute walk away. Immediately surrounding the estate, however, are olive groves, cultivated fields, and abundant woods that buffer it from the crowds and urban bustle. Situated on the road to Fiesole, north of Florence, Maiano also lies at the foot of the road leading to the source of the *pietra serena* stone used to construct Florence's magnificent churches San Lorenzo and Santo Spirito.

Today, the villa at Maiano hosts matrimonial festivities and houses a museum of interest to historians and film enthusiasts. The interior has been substantively preserved in the Victorian fashion of the late nineteenth century, and the ground floor's drawing room and dining room are recognizable as the setting of various interior shots in the Merchant Ivory film, *A Room with a View.*

The estate's office, *frantoio,* and shop selling local produce lie across a small road from the villa, updating a formerly cloistered medieval convent and ancient farm for current use. The Benedictine nuns' private living quarters, around the periphery of the convent's open courtyard, have been transformed into apartments and an artist's studio that restores fine textiles. While the *frantoio* continues its age-old production of the estate's high-quality olive oil, the farm workers' houses now offer vacationers "a room with a view," not only to Florence's majestic beauty, but to the serenity of her countryside in the hills just outside her doors.

VIEWS OF MAIANO
(opposite) Estate owner Lucrezia Miari Fulcis, in the villa's drawing room used in the film A Room with a View.
PAGE 24 CLOCKWISE FROM TOP LEFT *The living room of Le Colonne (the columns) apartment; Fattoria di Maiano's villa; The villa's view toward Florence.*

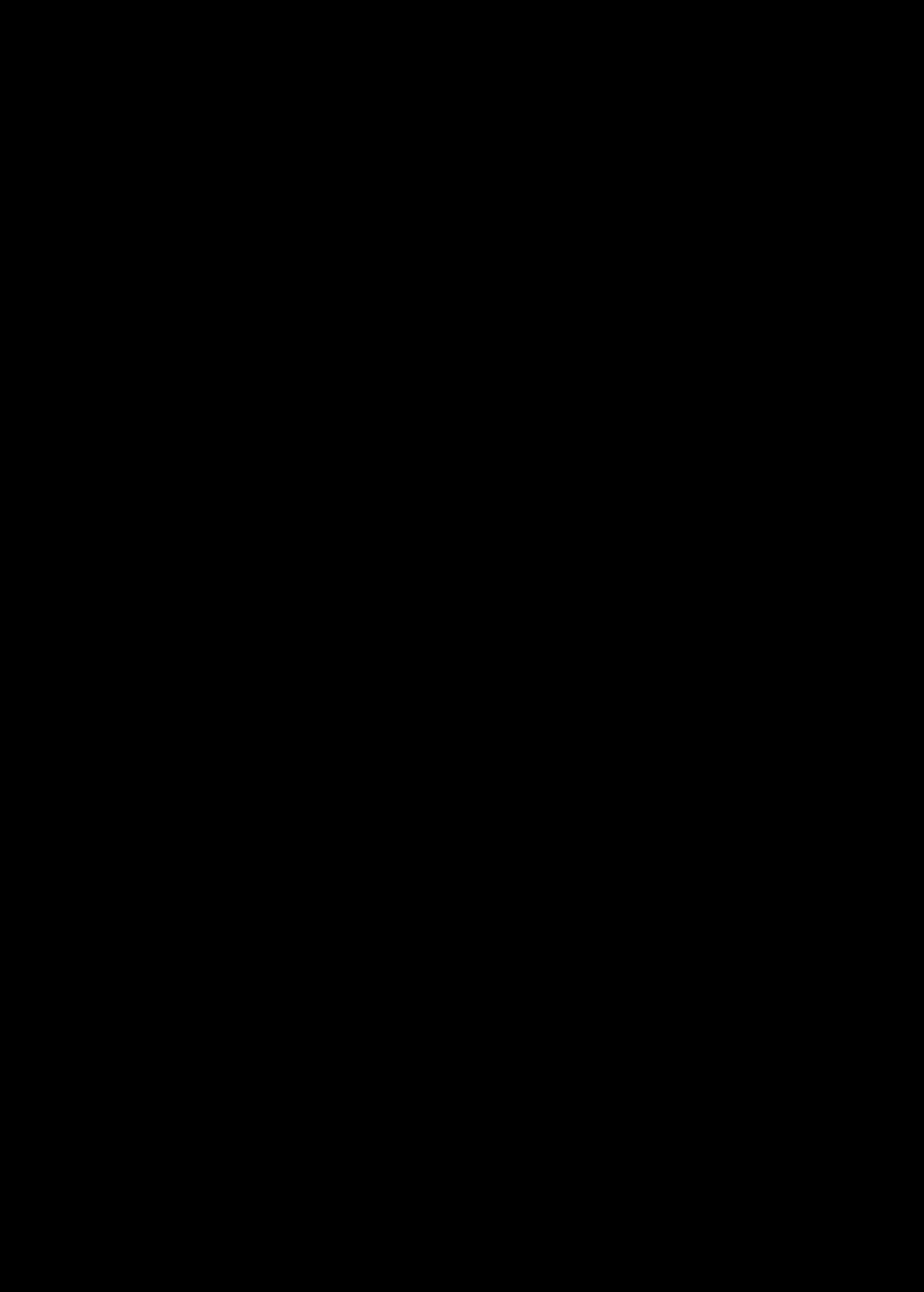

TENUTA DI CAPEZZANA

During the time of Charles the Great, specifically, December 16, 804 A.D., a priest of the area drew up a contract for a lease of "... a place called Capezzana, which was inhabited by the farmer Petruccio, with the house and its buildings and land, the courtyard, the gardens, the vineyards, the woods, the olive orchards, the cultivated and uncultivated fields...." This is the oldest written record of the Capezzana farm, and it demonstrates that wine and olive oil have been important to the life of the estate for more than eleven hundred years.

Not only has the Carmignano area produced wine for centuries, but the DOCG wines are also of a very high quality. In 1716, the Medici designated Carmignano one of four areas in Tuscany producing superior wine; the other three were the Val d'Arno (the Arno River Valley) and the Chianti and Pomino regions. Ugo Contini Bonacossi and his family continue the fine wine tradition today, producing eight wines, a *vin santo* (dessert wine),

VIEWS OF CAPEZZANA *(below) The interior courtyard of Villa Capezzana. (opposite)* Vin santo *grapes.* PAGE 28 *The cantina was sealed-off during World War II to protect the wine.* PAGE 29 *(above) A dining room where harvest dinners are held. (right) The large terra cotta pots are called* orci.

COr
97
28.4.9
CARMIGN

and three grappa varieties each year. The name of one of the wines, *Barco Reale* (literally, "Royal Property"), DOC, reflects the Medici influence—the family not only appreciated the area wine but also built the villa at Capezzana for one of the Medici daughters. In the rare case that the vineyard's production for fine wines does not meet the Contini Bonacossi family's high standards, they, instead of producing a lesser-quality fine wine, only use the grapes for the simpler wines that year. With this standard of excellence, the Carmignano wine legacy will continue well beyond the next generation of the Contini Bonacossis.

CHIANTI

THE QUINTESSENTIAL IMAGE OF TUSCANY IS PROBABLY MOST EMBODIED IN THE SIMPLE TERM "CHIANTI." FROM THE ARCHAIC STRAW-COVERED JUGS TO THE "SUPER TUSCANS" NOW CREATED IN THIS AREA, TO THE Strada Chiantigiana routes that traverse the countryside from Florence to Siena to Arezzo, wine colors our perception of this central region. Though the popularity of Italian wine in recent years has made Chianti available all over the world, there is still a simple pleasure in securing a table in a *trattoria,* delving into a pasta dish of homemade *pappardelle* with a *cinghiale* (wild boar) sauce or other gastronomic specialty and washing it down with a glass of locally produced Chianti. When driving along the wine routes in this region, stopping to taste and purchase wines from the estates is a treat not to be missed; it also offers a wonderful opportunity to become more familiar with the excellent olive oils produced here. Each region's microclimate, as well as the handling of the olives during production, affects the flavor of the oil. Once, olive oil was pressed from olives picked at prime ripeness and from those collected from the ground after falling from the trees. After the extensive research of recent years, however, experts have determined that the highest quality oil results from olives in their earliest stages of ripeness, and that "fallen" olives produce oil which exceeds acceptable naturally occurring acidity levels for extra virgin olive oil. Methods of cold-pressing the olives have evolved as well, though premium quality oils are still made by crushing olives with ancient granite stones, as well as by the newest ultra-modern means. As the debate among producers continues, the freshness and aroma of this emerald gold produced by various means, tasted at the site of production, will be long remembered.

VIEWS OF CHIANTI

(opposite) The vineyards of the Volpaia estate are surrounded by trees planted to enliven the winter landscape, while the severely pruned grapevines are dormant and listlessly await the warmth of spring. PAGE 32 *Chianti's undulating landscape.*

FATTORIA LE CORTI

It could be said that the owners of this estate, the Corsini family, helped settle America, as their ancestors owned the Mayflower before it set sail with its brave pilgrims. This noble Florentine family also produced a saint, St. Andrea Corsini, and a pope, Clement XII. It was Pope Clement XII who commissioned the famous Trevi Fountain in Rome (look for the Corsini coat of arms at the top of the fountain). The villa owes its present appearance to a complete remodeling at the beginning of the seventeenth century.

Duccio Corsini and his young family continue the commitment to the advancement of culture. As Duccio Corsini puts it, "We sell half a bottle of wine and half a bottle of culture"—not an empty motto. Many artistic and cultural events, held both in Le Corti and in the palaces in Florence, are sponsored by the Corsini family. Each September, *Giardini in Fiera,* one of Italy's most important flower and garden shows, takes place in Le Corti's eighteenth-century Italianate garden. For the past three years, the palazzo in Florence belonging to Duccio's parents, Filippo and Giorgiana Corsini, has hosted a show in its magnificent garden featuring Italian artisans and live exhibitions of bronze work, wigs and makeup, watchmaking, painting restoration, and other lesser-known art forms.

VIEWS OF LE CORTI

(below) The coats-of-arms painted onto the ceiling document the noble families that have married into the Corsini family over the last several hundred years. The villa's "wedding room," can be rented for wedding receptions. (opposite) The villa's Italianate garden. PAGE 36 *(top left) The villa of Le Corti. (lower left) Each autumn, the estate hosts an important flower show in its captivating garden.* PAGE 37 *Terra cotta pots are identified readily with the Italian countryside. These quiet giants are in the* orciaia, *a storage room where olive oil is traditionally kept on an estate from the moment the olives are pressed.*

CASTELLO DI BROLIO

VIEWS OF BROLIO

(opposite) The castle's entry is filled with age-old Ricasoli family antiques, acquired over the years since the family purchased the estate in 1141.

The Brolio castle, in various forms, has had a rather imposing presence in the Chianti countryside since the Ricasoli family purchased it in the early twelfth century. Its strategic position made it an important part of the line of defense between the arch-enemy city-states of Florence and Siena, which caused endless rebuilding. At the beginning of the Renaissance, fortified walls were built to protect it, just as the rival governments decided to settle their disputes and let area estates get back to the normal activities of making wine, olive oil, and other necessities. The massively elegant walls, built by architect and sculptor Sangallo at the beginning of the Renaissance, remain, jutting out of the annals of antiquity, to forever guard the peaceful vineyards below.

Brolio's winemaking began to get wide attention in the mid-1800s, when Bettino Ricasoli, a Prime Minister of Italy, invented the formula for Chianti wine there. Over one hundred years later, the family was selling the wine harvests to multinational companies, which annually bottled and sold several million bottles under the Brolio name.

In the 1990s, a member of the new generation, Francesco Ricasoli, gave up a successful commercial photography business to return to the estate with the intention of improving the now enormous wine production. In a dramatic managed buyout, the Ricasoli family regained control of Brolio's winemaking and, since 1993, has been reestablishing the estate's wines, reinvigorating them with the help of longtime friend and wine producer Filippo Mazzei, centuries of Ricasoli knowledge, and a healthy dose of modern methodology.

VIEWS OF BROLIO

(opposite) Brolio has an awesome, peaceful presence. This grand estate's tranquility and massive elegance attract savvy Italophiles, who flock to Brolio to see the magnificent castle, owned in the 1800s by Chianti wine "inventor" and onetime Italian Prime Minister Bettino Ricasoli—an ancestor of the current owner. (this page, left) The upstairs landing, leading to the castle's apartments. (below left) Brolio's owner today, Bettino Ricasoli, namesake of Chianti wine's famous founder. (below right) Detail of an apartment within the castle of Brolio.

CASTELLO DI CACCHIANO

The duality of the mythical god Bacchus (or Dionysus) is continuously evoked at the castle of Cacchiano in the land of Chianti Classico. Each year, the symbol of the god, the vines, offer up their bounty and are then severely pruned for the coming of winter, only to be revived by the warmth of spring. While symbolizing immortality, the God of the Vine was also characterized by fearless acts. The members of the family Ricasoli of Cacchiano reflected that bravery in their soldiering, inspiring the cry *"Dio ti Guardi da Cacchiano"* (God save you from the Cacchiano).

Like its neighboring cousin Brolio, winemaking dominates the activities of this estate. Vineyards cover the once embattled plain that unfolds at the feet of the *castello,* and feudal battles seem distant from the peaceful countryside. Looking out at the view, which has changed little in the castle's one thousand years of history, estate Manager Giovanni Ricasoli reflects, "I am happy that my generation is still able to enjoy this countryside; it remains unspoiled."

VIEWS OF CACCHIANO

(opposite) Cacchiano's castle and hamlet rise out of the countryside between the city of Siena and the Chianti Hills. (below left) Detail of a room in the rambling apartment Bindaccio, adjacent to the castle. The rooms are spread over three levels. (below right) The gateway topped with traditional finials welcomes visitors to the castle's garden.

FATTORIA CASTELLO DI BIBBIONE

The chapters of history can be read in the stone walls of the Bibbione castle, the foundations of which date to the ninth century. Centuries of renovation and rebuilding have left scars in the stone and masonry where ancient doors and windows once stood. Indeed, the castle has served many purposes in its long history: a medieval fortress, a sanctuary for pilgrims in the twelfth century, a Renaissance country home, and in 1511, the favorite hunting lodge of statesman and writer Niccolò Machiavelli. When the last of Machiavelli's direct descendants died in 1727, the Machiavelli name, estate, and noble title were passed to a cousin, who adopted the name Rangoni Machiavelli.

With over a thousand years of history, the castle has also accumulated its share of mystery and legend. A secret tunnel leads from the castle to the river plain below and was used to smuggle people and supplies to and from the estate during the wars of the Pesa River valley. During recent renovations, local masons surprised

VIEWS OF BIBBIONE *(opposite) Detail of the ancient castle's wall with sundial, window, and anchors—decorations on the ends of metal rods used to strengthen the medieval walls. (below) The castle and estate from a long, winding driveway below.* PAGE 46 *Bibbione's owners decorate the apartments with family belongings; here, a cupboard in a dining room.*

XII

the estate owners by breaking small holes in the walls; they claimed to be searching for the elusive golden-egg-laying chicken long associated with the castle.

Under the careful guidance of Antonella Rangoni Machiavelli, who combines strict attention to historical detail with a sensitivity to comforts of the modern world, the entire estate has been undergoing a painstaking renovation since 1985. Antonella Rangoni Machiavelli, in her commitment to restore the ancient beauty of the estate, wholeheartedly embraces one of the tenets of her illustrious ancestor, Niccolò, who said, "It is not titles that honor men, but men that honor titles."

VIEWS OF BIBBIONE

(above) Antonella Rangoni Machiavelli, the owner, and descendant of Niccolò Machiavelli.

CASTELLO DI FONTERUTOLI

The estate of Fonterutoli straddles the old border between the historically warring city-states of Florence and Siena. According to local folklore, the ever-fluctuating border was established near Fonterutoli thanks to a skinny black rooster. At the dawn of the Renaissance, it is said, the two city-states had grown weary of feuding and resolved to agree upon an official border between them. To determine the border, it was decided that one horseback rider would depart each city at the first crow of the rooster and each would ride toward the other until the two met. The meeting place would establish the territorial border.

Now, the people of Siena had on hand a plump, complacent bird, while the Florentines picked a nervous and hungry black rooster. The contented Sienese rooster settled into a peaceful sleep, waking the rider at first light. Florence's black rooster, however, due to its underfed and jittery disposition, nervously awoke the city's rider in the middle of the night. The next day, the people of Siena were confounded to discover that riders met a mere fifteen kilometers from their town—and forty-five kilometers from Florence. It is the familiar symbol of this black rooster that today commonly adorns bottles of Chianti wine.

Legend aside, the Fonterutoli estate has made quite a name for itself through its world-class wines. The Mazzei family, who have been the

proprietors of the estate since 1435, continues a long tradition of wine-making here.Brothers Francesco and Filippo Mazzei recently abandoned city life to return to Fonterutoli and manage the family trade. The brothers returned not only because of familial loyalty, but also for the sheer pleasure of country living. "This is a sort of paradise to us," Francesco says, "a wild place where, as boys growing up, we discovered the world." Recognizing a growing interest among tourists in Tuscan wine-making, the Mazzeis are keen to share their quiet, circumscribed world of this ancient country hamlet.

VIEWS OF FONTERUTOLI
PAGE 49 *A bell tower rises from the castle and hamlet of Fonterutoli. The hamlet is surrounded by the vineyards of this renowned wine estate.* THIS PAGE *(top right) Detail of the estate's wine cellar. (bottom right) An apartment with a loggia and a view. (below) Fonterutoli from a distance.* PAGE 51 *The Mazzei family crest adorns an iron gate.*

CASTELLO DI VOLPAIA

Though the fortifications of Volpaia no longer exist, the scarred stone walls tell us that this town, at one time, mounted a stout defense against invasions and occupation. War and invasion, of course, were common features of medieval life. What set this village apart was the fact that its formidable ramparts served to protect common villagers, not the lords of a noble family. People born in the village took its name *(della Volpaia),* and the hamlet survives as a testament to their ability to survive—and indeed to thrive—without the protection of a noble family. One villager, Lorenzo della Volpaia (1446–1512), earned renown for his skill in crafting fine instruments, including navigational aids and timepieces; several of his finely wrought sundials can still be found in collections in the United States and Europe. Lorenzo's son wrote a book on instrument-making that became a very important record of Renaissance times.

The medieval charm of this village, however, belies the trappings of modern agriculture that can be found within: behind the walls of a thirteenth-century church sit gleaming, silver tanks brimming with wine, and around the corner, behind unmarked doors, a state-of-the-art olive press, in the *frantoio,* silently awaits the November olive harvest. Maintaining the town's historic beauty is seen to by Giovannella Stianti, whose father purchased the hamlet for her as a wedding present in 1966. Soon after, Giovannella's father began to plant trees, and the family has since added three thousand cypresses to the grounds (the trees serve to break up the view of endless vineyards and farmland). Giovannella inherited from her father an appreciation of his philosophy of improving the "architectural landscape of agriculture." To that end, Giovannella and her family are creating within the village a vertical rose garden that will eventually include one hundred and fifty climbing roses.

VIEWS OF VOLPAIA

(opposite) The formerly fortified village of Volpaia is a beautiful hilltop town that successfully conceals any sign of the modern world.

VIEWS OF VOLPAIA *(clockwise from top left) "The temple of wine." Wine ferments in a deconsecrated thirteenth-century church; Detail of the hamlet; the eighteenth-century church is the most recent of three; Grapes drying to make* vin santo, *or "wine of saints." (right) Giovannella Stianti, seated in front of her frescoed portrait, painted in the early years of her marriage.*

TENUTA DI PETROLO

VIEWS OF PETROLO
(opposite) Lemon trees like this one, when not soaking up the Tuscan sun, are housed in a stone greenhouse called a limonaia. *(below) The estate's eleventh-century* pieve, *or parish church, with works of art by the Della Robbia family.*

The dominant feature of the Petrolo estate, which rises 1,500 feet above the surrounding plain, is the tower of Galatrona. Its lofty perch made the tower an important signaling station between Florence and Siena from the thirteenth to sixteenth century. Though the castle that accompanied the tower during the Middle Ages has not survived, Galatrona's ruin remains an instantly recognizable landmark in this region nestled between the hills of Chianti and the Arno River.

The tower now stands vigil over the Petrolo estate's present-day villa and its vineyards and olive groves, which belong to Lucia Sanjust Bazzocchi, who has overseen

the property since 1985. The 650 acres of woods that encircle Petrolo's cultivated lands enclose the estate's inhabitants in a cloak of tranquility. In the shadow of the watchful tower, it is easy to recede from the outside world; the serenity of the landscape is punctuated only by the comings and goings of the workers who tend to the estate's vineyards and olive groves. Indeed, wine-making has occupied the estate's various owners for centuries, possibly as early as Etruscan times though certainly from the 1200s, when local records reported that wines from the "big tower" were being exported to England. Petrolo also produces a superior olive oil, which meets the high standards of the Laudemio consortium and which is sold throughout Europe.

Nestled among the estate's vineyards and olive groves is the eleventh century *pieve* of St. John the Baptist, an important Romanesque parish church owned by the Vatican. The Church took particular interest in the prosperous estate at Galatrona, which it recognized as an excellent source of tax revenue. Today, the parish church is of interest to art historians; the church's magnificent art works are attributed to sculptors belonging to the renowned della Robbia family. Among the treasures are an ornate baptismal font attributed to Andrea della Robbia, a statue of San Giovanni Battista by Luca della Robbia, and a Eucharist cup by Giovanni della Robbia.

VIEWS OF PETROIO

(opposite) The ruin of the ancient tower of Galatrona. THIS PAGE*(below left) Typical of autumn, the* colorino *vineyards brighten the landscape. One of the olive trees of the Petrolo estate, which consistently produces olive oil of excellent quality, meeting the strict standards of the Chianti-based Laudemio association. (below right) Petrolo's villa and estate from above.*

CASTELLO DI POGGIO PETROIO

The Castle of Poggio Petroio has a history of inspired inhabitants. In the 900s, the property was given, as a dowry, to Camilla degli Aldobrandini's husband, who was of the Visdomini family. Their union produced a son named Giovanni Gualberto Visdomini, later canonized as San Giovanni Gualberto. The story says that the young man from Petroio was journeying to avenge his brother's murder, when in a moment of spiritual need, he knelt in front of a crucifix and asked for guidance. The head of Jesus on the crucifix turned to him, which dissuaded him from committing the murder. He went on to devote his life to religion and founded the Order of the Vallombrosani. Gualberto is remembered not only in a beautiful fresco at Poggio Petroio but also in Passignano, where his mortal remains are kept, as well as in a chapel dedicated to his memory at the Santa Trinita Church in Florence and in Dante Alighieri's writings.

In the 1960s, Elena Gioia and her husband Achille Alessandro Conti moved their family into Petroio's early-seventeenth-century villa. Conti spent time showing his champion dogs and, along the way, collecting dog curios. Upon his return to the estate one evening, he gazed up at the unused medieval tower in the villa's courtyard and decided to share his passion for dogs by exhibiting his extraordinary collection there. Today, the museum's collection has grown beyond Conti's own treasures—it includes donations from the British royal family and noble families of Italy as well as gifts from dog lovers all over the world.

VIEWS OF PETROIO

(opposite) The estate's iron gate opens onto the medieval tower, which houses Italy's first dog museum.

VIEWS OF PETROIO

(above left) Achille Alessandro Conti, founder of the museum, with a piece from the collection. (above right) The apartment walls are medieval and are embedded with Etruscan stone. (left) A fresco adorning an exterior wall, commemorating San Giovanni Gualberto, who was born here in the tenth century. (opposite) Conti is also a painter; the apartments are decorated with his elaborate trompe l'oeil *work.*

VILLA VISTARENNI

VIEWS OF VISTARENNI *(opposite) A detail of the villa's Venetian glass windows.* PAGE 66 *The name Vistarenni comes from the Etruscan word* Fistarinne, *or "fine view." The villa's majestic Venetian facade also becomes a "fine view" from the road below.* PAGE 67 *Vistarenni's wine cellar, carved out of the subterranean stone, uses traditional wooden barrels to store the wine.*

The Venetian facade of Villa Vistarenni stands out in the Tuscan landscape like an elegant foreigner. In the late 1800s, Giorgio Sonnino bought the eighteenth-century Renaissance-style villa and endowed it with its present Venetian character, complete with sweeping front staircases and Venetian glass windows.

Elisabetta Tognana, the current owner and native of Venice, brings her own personal influence to the Vistarenni estate. Before entering the world of Chianti wine culture, Tognana was already challenging traditional barriers as a race car driver. In 1980, she took control of Vistarenni without any knowledge of wine making at all. Immersing herself in the traditions of Chianti and Tuscany, Tognana rapidly developed her wine-making skills, and by 1987 had won an award for her wine.

Having established herself in the region, Tognana discovered that many other women were involved in viniculture, but that their presence in the industry was practically invisible. Thus, in 1987, she formed an association entitled *Le Donne del Vino,* or "The Women of Wine." Since the first meeting, membership has grown from 50 to 250 women, representing not only wine makers, but restaurant and *enoteca* owners, sommeliers, and wine journalists.

At Villa Vistarenni, Elisabetta Tognana introduced an outsider's view and wove it seamlessly into the time-honored traditions of Chianti. She and her young family once adored the Tuscan landscape from a distance—now, they have made it their own.

CASTELLO DI MONTALTO

A surprise was waiting in the Castle of Montalto, a former fortress of Berardenga, for an unsuspecting Italian man and his American-born wife in 1970. The couple was searching for a country cottage, and on a whim visited the castle, which happened to be for sale. Upon their arrival, they discovered that the owners of the castle, the last of the Palmieri family, were the distant cousins of the gentleman. The Palmieri had owned the property since 1512, and a deal was quickly struck to keep the castle in the family. It became the full-time residence for the city-weary couple, who in turn carefully restored and preserved the castle, its outbuildings and the many frescoes in the house.

In the course of the past thirty years, they have discovered that castle living has unusual challenges. One year, for example, a fire threatened to ruin forever a frescoed room in the large tower living room. The heat of the blaze had melted a plastic dollhouse, turning the walls of the frescoed room completely black. The Tuscan countryside

VIEWS OF MONTALTO

(opposite) A long, narrow driveway lined with clipped hedges opens suddenly, revealing the fairytale castle of Montalto. (below) Detail of the fresco saved by Tuscan bread.

transplants tried cleaning the walls with water and other cleaning solutions, to no avail. Finally, they were given a piece of age-old Tuscan wisdom—bread should do the trick. The saltless bread had been used for centuries in candle-smoke-blackened churches and quickly removed the walls' smoke damage without affecting the beautiful artwork beneath it. The owners have developed a harmonious blend between old and new; they have honored the hundreds of years of Montalto's history while adding their own stories along the way.

Artwork is to be found all over the Montalto estate. When the Palmieri family acquired the fortress in the early sixteenth century, they changed its demeanor from a fortified protector of Berardenga to a home, through Renaissance decoration and porticos. The fresco above the entrance gate, on the interior of the courtyard, depicts the story of the namesake of *dio di San Martino,* which is the time of year during November when the fall temperatures break and give a summer-like respite from the cold ahead.

They also used their family's symbol, the *cinghiale* as an adornment on many of the stone decorations in the courtyard.

VIEWS OF MONTALTO

(opposite) The former stable and granary have been beautifully restored. (below) The Palmieri family symbol was the fierce cinghiale, *or wild boar, found in abundance in the countryside.*

MONTALCINO AND THE VAL D'ORCIA

THE ANCIENT ROAD TO ROME ONCE TRAVELED BY THE PENITENT IS NOW THE BUSTLING CASSIA (SS2) WHICH, DEPARTING FROM SIENA, MEANDERS THROUGH THE DENUDED CRETE HILLS, AND 40 MILES south, the deeply hewn Orcia and Asso river valleys. This area of central Tuscany counts among its treasures the walled medieval city of Montalcino and the heralded renaissance jewel of Pienza. Built in 1460 by Pope Pius II (the first of two Popes from the noble Piccolomini family, whose symbol, the crescent moon, adorns hundreds of buildings in the region), the town of Pienza is distinguished by its relative modernity from the neighboring medieval towns. This captivating region within Tuscany is well known for its sulfurous, geothermal waters, which beckon to the aching muscles of visitors. For spiritual soothing, the early twelfth-century Romanesque Abbey of Sant'Antimo is open to the public, tended by Gregorian-chanting monks. The dramatic countryside inspires long walks along the clearly marked paths traversing the landscape. Rising on the southern horizon, the graceful Monte Amiata welcomes winter skiers as well as mushroom and chestnut hunters in the fall. The mighty red wine, *Brunello di Montalcino,* and its cousin *Rosso di Montalcino,* are products of this Colli Senesi outcropping of Chianti. They accompany the area's special foods: fennel-cured pork, *pici* (egg-less pasta), *scottiglia* (savory meats, simmered in herbs, tomatoes and olive oil) and *niveggiolo,* a soft cheese served between fern leaves.

VIEWS OF MONTALCINO *(clockwise from top left) Sheep graze among the Crete Hills; The sentinel to the south, Monte Amiata.; The Abbey of Sant'Antimo; Hunters are common during the autumn months.* PAGES 74–75 *A line of trees punctuates this heavily cultivated region.*

IL CASTELLO DI RIPA D'ORCIA

Overlooking the Orcia River valley, three miles from San Quirico d'Orcia, the fortified castle and hamlet of Ripa are within minutes of two noted wine areas: the Brunello di Montalcino and Vino Nobile di Montepulciano. The name Ripa d'Orcia, which derives from *ripa,* meaning "steep," and the Orcia River, proves highly appropriate; the long, ramparted castle wall is built on a cliff, the sheer face of which plunges dramatically into the river valley below. The view across the valley displays a wild, natural area protected by the local government. This vast and unspoiled setting creates the secluded, country retreat character that encompasses Ripa d'Orcia.

The entrance to the castle is a magnificent battlement gate, hearkening back to warring times; though the first written record of its existence dates to the beginning of the 1300s, the castle was probably built during the early Middle Ages. The Piccolomini family obtained the estate in 1438, and its present owner, Laura Aluffi Pentini, is a descendant of this noble family.

Historically, the hamlet and its property provided virtually everything the castle and its inhabitants required, from spiritual needs, addressed in the church, to corporal necessities such as cheeses, wool, fruits, livestock and freshly pressed olive oil. As a reminder of days past, the owners have fashioned a table from a grinding stone formerly used to crush the olives. Though the feudal system is long gone, the enclosed hamlet hotel continues to feel quietly self-contained while its protective castle walls provide a welcoming refuge from the bustling modern world.

VIEWS OF RIPA D'ORCIA
(right) Inside of the castle gates, the drive winds uphill among the many dépendences, *the dependent buildings of the castle, whose residents once provided for every need within the hamlet.* PAGE 78 *A view from the castle to the neighboring natural reserve.* PAGE 79 *(above) The beautiful, though poisonous, oleander bush bends in the wind, in front of the hamlet's chapel. (below) An arched "museum" under the castle houses age-old treasures, like the loom in the foreground.*

LA FOCE

The sprawling estate of La Foce was purchased by Antonio and Iris Origo in 1924. The couple had been searching for a place in which they could do "a lifetime of work," and they found it on this 2,200-acre property, which consists of vast tracts of cultivated and wild land, fifty-three individual farmhouses, the fifteenth-century former inn that lends the estate its name, and the nearby castle—Castellucio. To both the estate and the people who farmed it, the Origos brought renewed energy and a passionate sense of purpose—both in their desire to improve the social conditions of the men and women who worked on this land and in their mission to improve the agricultural practices on the farm. To these ends, they built a hospital, a school, and an orphanage; they rebuilt the tenant farmers' houses; they reforested the property; and they instituted land reform.

VIEWS OF LA FOCE

(right) The apartments' antique furnishings were originally in the villa at La Foce.

Today, Donata and Benedetta Origo and their families continue the traditions of their parents and have woven their own artistic legacy into the natural and man-made tapestry of this vast estate. The farmhouses and other buildings on the estate have been meticulously restored and refurnished. Castelluccio hosts a chamber music festival each summer, in addition to arts exhibitions and courses. In between events, visitors are invited to peruse Castellucio's library or relax at the wine bar. Cecil Pinset's extensive garden at La Foce is now considered a regional treasure; it is comprised of elaborate formal rooms in the Italianate style, which give way here and there to rose and lemon gardens, fountains, sculpture, and carefully planned vistas of the surrounding countryside. La Foce, which began in 1498 as an inn for travelers following the busy road to Rome, has today become—thanks to the Origo family—a serene oasis where visitors can steep themselves in the beauty and artistic pleasures of the Tuscan countryside.

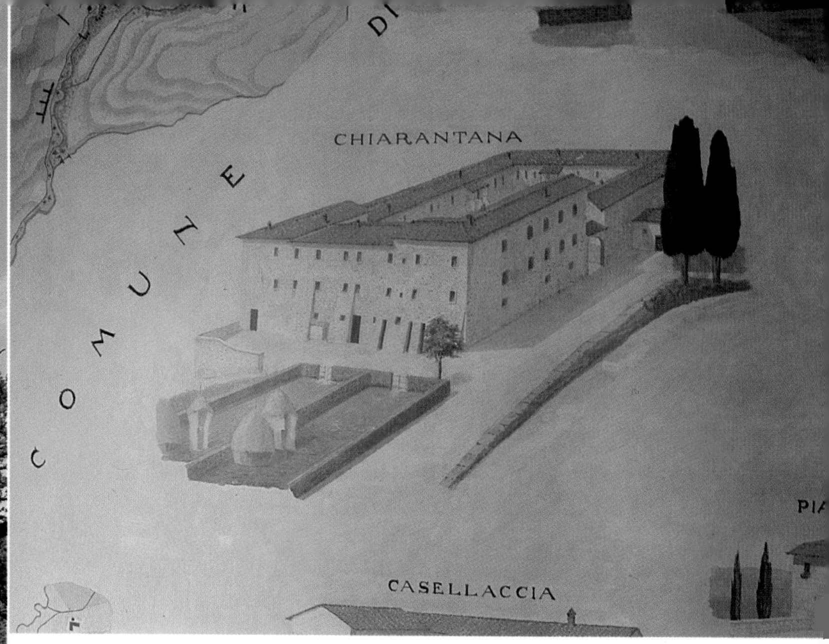

VIEWS OF LA FOCE

(above) Detail of a fresco inside the former inn of La Foce. The rendering depicts the entire estate; the building pictured is La Chiarentana. (above left) The contemporary garden surrounding this house named Montauto was designed by landscape designer Oliva di Collobiano. (below left) Benedetta Origo.

PAGE 83 *Iris Origo, the internationally known historian and biographer, planted this row of cypress trees to view from her window. Her books on the Orcia River Valley are excellent reading on the social history of the area.*

LUCIGNANELLO BANDINI

There are many spectacular views of Tuscany, but from this tiny hamlet of Lucignano d'Asso, the unadulterated expanse of the rolling Sienese Crete hills, surrounding hill towns, river valleys, and mountains is a remarkable sight. From the village's highest point—the site of a swimming pool—one takes in a full three hundred and sixty degree range of pristine Tuscany, but from virtually any position within the hamlet, the view is equally arresting. In addition to its view, this area is notable for its soil, which makes it one of the few locations in the world ideal for the natural growth of

VIEWS OF LUCIGNANELLO BANDINI

(opposite) A stone lion guards the entrance to the hamlet's protected inner piazzale *(small stone courtyard) and two of its three charming apartments. (below) The view of the surrounding landscape over the church's rooftop.*

the elusive white truffle. White truffles are rare indeed, and the nearby town of San Giovanni d'Asso has a special truffle festival in mid-November to celebrate its good fortune. After gathering all the truffles found by each specially trained hunter, or *tartufaio,* the festival culminates with a dinner in the *piazza* below the castle, and the largest white truffle of the season, called the "Truffle of Peace," is awarded to an international leader.

The two sisters who run the Lucignanello Bandini estate are extremely knowledgeable about truffles and their culinary uses and will even go so far as to reveal their delectable secrets (their cardinal rule: "never cook them"). They are equally passionate about the countryside and willingly share their extensive knowledge about the surrounding area; the sisters take pleasure in welcoming those adventurous visitors who come to discover their favorite piece of the world.

VIEWS OF LUCIGNANELLO BANDINI

(left) Careful driving skills are required to negotiate the narrow arched passageway leaving the estate. (right) Well-appointed kitchens are characteristic of the accommodations at Lucignanello Bandini; this particular house is called Casa Remo.

FATTORIA DI COSONA

The name Cosona can be traced to the Etruscan period, and evidence of a long succession of castles and buildings erected on this site bears witness to an extensive material history as well. The Cosona estate and its predecessors have defended this strategically important site over the centuries from attacks by territorial cities in both Tuscany and Umbria. In modern times, Cosona was invaded during World War II, and all of the area's inhabitants were forced into the ancient parish church, which had long been considered the "mother church" of the region. The estate currently consists of a palazzo, dating from the early fifteenth century, and a group of converted farmhouses. The owner, probably because of his extensive knowledge and enthusiasm for history, makes a point to maintain the rustic character of the farmhouses, which overlook the resplendent valley between the Asso and Tuoma rivers. Cosona's proprietors obviously recognize the importance placed on maintaining tradition in this part of the country; after all, their family has shared the same breathtaking view of the valley with the family that owns the nearby estate of Lucignanello Bandini for over five hundred years.

VIEWS OF COSONA

OPPOSITE *The Cosona estate's hilltop perch, just outside the beautiful town of Pienza, overlooks the Tuoma and Asso River valleys. (left) The palazzo and well at Cosona. The owner's family has enjoyed the expansive view from this outdoor courtyard for over five hundred years.*

CASTELLO ROMITORIO

The estate of Castello Romitorio consists of a hidden castle, an artistic cantina, a former water mill, and a number of farmhouses. Molino, the ancient water mill, has been recently restored; it was most likely built during the twelfth century. The water that had originally powered the mill's machinery once again rushes under and around the building, now converted to a luxurious rental house. One of the farmhouses, *Poggio di Sopra,* has also enjoyed a careful restoration, and now contains three distinctive apartments. Surrounding both residences are extensive grounds including gardens, olive groves, and vineyards.

In their current state, the houses offer no hint of their former purposes subordinate to the castle. Both had functioned under the feudal system of *mezzadria,* or tenant farming, which continued in some form throughout Italy until the 1960s. Under this system, the resident farmer handed over half his crops to the proprietor who owned both the land and the machinery. Today farm life here continues to flourish, though now utilizing modern systems while focusing on the production of fewer, more lucrative crops.

VIEWS OF ROMITORIO

(below left) Molino, the ancient water mill at Romitorio. (below right) Vineyards and stunning scenery surround Romitorio's castle. (right) Alessandro Chia, the estate's owner, is also the artist who designed this eclectic wine cellar. PAGE 92 *Poggio di Sopra enjoys a view of the river valleys and hills between Monte Amiata and the medieval town of Montalcino.* PAGE 93 *The long table awaits friends, relatives, and grape pickers in celebration of the wine harvest.*

NORTHWESTERN TUSCANY

FOLLOWING A COURSE HUGGING TUSCANY'S WESTERN COAST, THIS AREA OF ESTATES BEGINS IN THE NORTHERN APENNINE (OR APPUANE) ALPS, WENDS ITS WAY THROUGH THE HOMETOWN OF PUCCINI—the walled town of Lucca—past Pisa's leaning tower, and on toward the forest of citadels at San Gimignano. As in the rest of this verdant region, vineyards and olive trees cover the hills, though the terrain here is interrupted by chestnut trees, fields of golden wheat, and white mounds of alabaster. The Aurelia, the old coastline road, meanders slowly along the edge of the Mediterranean Sea to the west, in search of undiscovered treasures. Along the way, friendly locals are more than willing to help with directions to a favorite trattoria. In summer, the Etruscan Riviera is a sunbather's mecca; seaside resorts are interspersed with Etruscan sites and natural reserves. Further inland, the scenic, twisting road toward Volterra, referred to as the Volterrana, turns and twists past some of Tuscany's most arresting views. Much of Tuscany's southern coastal plain was once known primarily for its swamps and mosquitoes, and was dismissed as uninhabitable until very recent times. Only in the last two hundred years has the land been reclaimed, and seen outside development. While Lucca to the north has always enjoyed a reputation for the finest olive oils, her neighbors to the south have only recently received accolades for their fine, climate-defying extra virgin olive oil. The tiny hamlet of Bolgheri is home to several excellent-quality olive oil producers who also create a number of Italy's finest wines, including Ornellaia, Sassicaia, and Grattamacco. The picturesque hamlet of Castagneto Carducci takes its name from the poet who immortalized the impressive cypress lane here rising from the scrub of the expansive seacoast.

NORTHWESTERN TUSCANY
The countryside connects its precious towns together in an architectural necklace: (clockwise from upper left) Inside the town of Lucca; San Gimignano's medieval towers; A church in Casale Marittimo.

VILLA OLIVA-BUONVISI

Villa Oliva-Buonvisi, nestled in the Luccese Hills above the walled city of Lucca, dates back to the late 1400s. The classic Luccan villa has two grand sides with accompanying entrances. The back entrance is comprised of a two-story loggia and massive, one-piece columns formed of Pietra di Matraia, a quarried stone used to build much of the city of Lucca. The front of the villa has an imposing approach which rises from the gate to the front door; the long, inclined driveway was created so that the looming villa would impress the owner's importance upon approaching guests.

The magnificent garden was created in the 1700s and has evolved over the past three hundred years. Today's garden graces the estate with the eternal murmur of fountains, the cool shade of ancient trees, vast expanses of lawn surrounding isolated explosions of blooming color, a grove of eucalyptus trees, a fanciful swimming pool, a hidden *limonaia,* and a tennis court. The garden even has a legend—it is said that the mermaid fountain is the result of a doomed relationship. A young lady, who was an occupant of the villa and who believed in the "mystic arts," fell in love with a fisherman. The young man's family didn't approve of the match because of her unusual beliefs and practices; the young woman's wealthy family didn't approve of the marriage because of his social status. Meanwhile, an inquisition guaranteed that she would likely be a target of severe punishment, due to her beliefs. To ensure their eternal togetherness, the young woman turned herself and her lover into the stone figures of the fountain, where they will forever remain united—if not in stone, then in legend.

VIEWS OF BUONVISI *(opposite) The front entrance of the villa presides over several acres of garden, in bloom much of the year.* PAGE 100 *An exterior view of one of the estate's apartments.* PAGE 101 *(upper left) Detail of the fountain of the mermaid and her lover. (upper right) A marble water trough in what was, at one time, a very elegant stable. (below) From the rear garden, the back view of the villa, with its grand, two-story arched loggia.* PAGES 96–97 *The scenic countryside of the Volterrana*

PERALTA

Thirty minutes from Lucca, carved into the side of a mountain between the Apuane Alps and the Ligurian Sea, is the tiny hamlet of Peralta. Having braved the increasingly narrow road through the woods by car, leaving it in a parking lot below, one continues the ascent to Peralta on foot. The comfortable walk, among the olive and chestnut trees, shows off the dramatic scenery of the mountainside above, as well as the steep slope below. After a few minutes walk, the path, guarded by a split-rail fence, opens onto the hamlet's small square a half mile from the car; the houses are built vertically above the square and the path's fence becomes the guard rail for the piazza, with a view over a large bronze sculpture and out to the mountains and the sea beyond.

In the piazza one finds a sculpture of a phoenix, created by the estate's owner, Fiore de Henriquez, who for thirty years has been engaged here, producing her own art as well as collaborating with local artisans who have managed to coax the original beauty out of Peralta. The creative remodeling includes not only the houses, but the outdoor eating area, nestled into the olive grove below the piazza, and the swimming pool at the end of a natural stone stairway above the village's houses. The estate maintains the feeling of a relaxed arts retreat of sorts; an open, friendly atmosphere dominates and the many beautiful sculptures of Peralta's hostess invite calm contemplation.

VIEWS OF PERALTA

(opposite) The owner's artistic style is reflected in the apartments. The table pictured here is fashioned from a huge gear, and her sculpture enhances the room.

VIEWS OF PERALTA

(above) From below, Peralta's tower marks the hamlet's position on the side of the mountain. (right) Nets are usually a tool of convenience during olive harvest; Peralta's steep inclines necessitate their use.

VILLA DEL MONTE

Just inside Siena's territorial border with Florence, the estate of Villa del Monte rises above the bucolic, emerald countryside. The formal tiers of medieval towers (one square and the other round), as well as the villa's Italianate garden and elaborate staircase surrounded by eighteenth-century walls emerge gracefully from the rolling hills, planted with cypress and pines, olive groves and vineyards.

Framed by the renovated square tower's arched windows, the neighboring city of San Gimignano is a fine example of a medieval city, providing an impressive vista with its signature forest of towers rising from its tiny girth.

VIEWS OF VILLA DEL MONTE

(opposite) A tier of gardens surrounds Villa del Monte's main villa. The square tower to the left has been refurbished as an apartment for two. (below left) Detail of a fireplace and screen in an apartment within the villa complex. (below right) A view of the countryside just outside of the estate's front gate.

FATTORIA DI MONTEGEMOLI

One vaguely salty spring is all that remains of the *moie* (salt springs) that the castle of Montegemoli fought to protect over the first several centuries of its presence along the Cecina River near the western coast of Tuscany. In the long days predating electricity and refrigeration, the springs of this area were prized for their extracted salt, used to cure meat. Today, driving to Montegemoli along the Volterrana, the scenic road toward the town of Volterra, the outcroppings of alabaster in the landscape of wheat fields is more likely to catch the eye for its singular visual effect. The golden fields produce a grain used in the renowned, toothsome bread fired in the ovens below the castle and in pasta used all over Italy. The grain is such an important part of the region's economy that the castle has been used in part as a granary since the early 1800s.

VIEWS OF MONTEGEMOLI

(opposite) Freshly-baked Pane di Montegemoli *is delivered throughout Tuscany every day. Each loaf, made from grain grown around this village, weighs almost five pounds. (below) Montegemoli's church casts a shadow across the circular piazza and onto one end of the castle complex. These three floors, formerly a school and storage rooms, now house the estate's three apartments.*

At one end of the hamlet, across a circular piazza—the footprint of one of the castle's former towers—the Romanesque church of San Bartolomeo is rumored to be the baptismal place of Dante Alighieri, the most celebrated of Italian poets. Though not confirmed by any official source, research is being conducted by a local priest who believes that Dante's mother was from Montegemoli. Another scholar, a Boston art historian, has recently attributed a painting inside the church to fourteenth century painter and pupil of Maestro Giotto, Francesco Neri Guintarini.

VIEWS OF MONTEGEMOLI

(below) Inside the church, this alabaster font, or acquasantiera, *is decorated with the coat of arms of the Incontri family of Volterra. (opposite) The hamlet and castle of Montegemoli.*

FATTORIA DI MONTELOPIO

Flanked by the Era and Roglio rivers, the tiny village of Montelopio lies north of San Gimignano, twenty miles from the Etruscan Riviera. Through a small door behind an unassuming wall, the unexpected grandeur of this villa and farm is revealed. The Mazzetti family has owned and lived in this olive oil- and wine-producing estate for three hundred years. Originally, these buildings belonged to a large farm, famous for its table olives. In medieval times, the mansion was owned by the order of the Malta and later was given by the city of Florence as a reward to Pietro Gaetani, a member of a historical family from Pisa, upon switching his loyalty from his home city to the feudal power of Florence. Since then, the estate has changed hands a number of times until at last falling into the possession of the current owners.

VIEWS OF MONTELOPIO

(below) This grand coat of arms marks the country estate, which looks out to the olive trees and the vast country–side beyond its protective wall. (opposite) The villa, tower and adjacent apartment have been historically preserved according to the vincolo, *legal guidelines for changing and renovating historical structures. Thanks to these carefully observed stipulations, the glory of homes and estates like Montelopio has survived the centuries. Here, a living room in the apartment is decorated with the family's photographs. (The front cover of this book features a view of the villa's exterior.)*

UMBRIA

UMBRIA HAS YET TO ACHIEVE THE INTERNATIONAL RENOWN OF NEIGHBORING REGION TUSCANY, THOUGH HER ORVIETO CLASSICO WINE IS ENJOYED THE WORLD OVER. THIS QUIET, UNSPOILED province southeast of Tuscany, bisected by the Tevere River, offers a veritable bounty to those willing to venture a bit inland to discover her charms. Orvieto, in western Umbria, lends its name not only to a notable wine region, but also to a hill town with a magnificent thirteenth-century cathedral worth taking a detour to visit. Assisi, synonymous with its St. Francis, is a sacred destination for those who seek a celebration of the natural world; the town, protected by law from indiscriminate development, is subject to change only by nature's hand and has retained the same character for nearly three-quarters of a millennium. Summer brings the highly acclaimed *Festival of Two Worlds* to Spoleto and Italy's most important jazz festival, *Umbria Jazz,* to Perugia. Ceramics aficionados flock to Deruta to purchase twice-fired *majolica* pottery, painted with designs of Renaissance times. The gastronomic tradition of Umbria relies on simply-prepared fresh foods. Pork is the meat of choice, though game birds frequent the *secondi,* or second plate, menu. Black truffles and delicate white-flowered lentils abound in the outlying areas, and Umbrian children (and adults) dream of chocolates from Perugia. *Bruschetta,* or bread toasted with olive oil and rubbed with garlic, is common in many regions in Italy, but in Umbria it reaches its pinnacle, celebrated in a festival in the village of Spello. Lovers of history will find the footprints of times past; from the well-preserved Etruscan site at Amelia, the legendary Roman-Carthaginian battle-grounds surrounding Lake Trasimeno to the thieving parade of Napoleonic armies, Umbria has provided a stage on which both her favorite sons and murderous invaders have made their indelible marks.

UMBRIA

(opposite) Spello, a hilltop town in Umbria between Foligno and Perugia, offers visitors a host of attractions, from its well-preserved Roman portals, to well-prepared bruschetta, *the centerpiece of a feast held in late winter.* PAGES 116 & 117 *Todi's profile through morning's mist.*

CASTELLO DI PETROIA

On the border between the territories of Perugia and Gubbio, and hidden in the thick woodlands overlooking the Chiasco valley, lies the twelfth-century castle of Petroia. Much of the history of this beautifully restored estate is tied to Perugia and Gubbio, two Umbrian arch-rival territories of feudal times. The dominant, square, eleventh-century tower on the property appears rather forbidding; the only entrance is from an exterior staircase, which rises more than a story before reaching the door to the landing. Once inside, however, the feeling changes; an unusual apartment on four levels has been fashioned out of the entire tower. The renovation of this estate follows ancient tradition. The carpentry is done in-house, and the wood used is harvested from the surrounding acreage. The decor inside the common rooms reflects the years of the castle's history; the giant chandeliers look medieval—only the light bulbs give away a more recent fabrication. Above the castle, the large, airy loggia is a special treat; breezes dance through the giant pines enclosing the loggia, offering welcome respite from the summer heat.

VIEWS OF PETROIA

(below) The fortified castle and hamlet of Petroia withstood periodic wars and occupations before the Renaissance. In 1422, Count Federico, son of Guidantonio and future Duke of Urbino, was born here. In 1909, it was purchased by the Sagrini family, and remains in their possession today. (opposite) Detail of a living room in the Petroia castle.

FATTORIA DI TITIGNANO

The Titignano estate's perch, on a hilltop in the wilds of western Umbria, gives it a changing character throughout the seasons. The altitude as well as the fresh breezes chasing across the plains below offer a respite from the summer heat, while, during the winter months, the haunting winds lend a mysterious character to this former palace of the Counts of Montemarte.

Regardless of the season, the morning sun illuminates Titignano's sweeping view which extends to two provinces and is punctuated by the hill towns of Todi and

VIEWS OF TITIGNANO

(opposite) Titignano is known throughout the region for its memorable food. Here, pasta dough is rolled before cutting. (below) The uninterrupted pristine setting of the hamlet; the estate's pool is artfully tucked away below this wall.

Orvieto. From the *piazzale* (the village's small stone courtyard), in drier seasons, submerged farmhouses may rise mysteriously from the Lago di Corbara.

A sure way to overcome any weather is to step inside Titignano's castle for an evening in the frescoed, *trompe l'oeil* dining room. There you'll enjoy a meal memorable for the marriage of fresh foods produced on the estate, and the formidable culinary skills of the resident chefs. The recipes and menus are from owner Nerina Incisa della Rocchetta's ancestors and have been served for generations. The seasonal foods determine each day's menu; throughout the year diners are rewarded with *cinghiale* (wild boar), pasta with truffle sauce, salumi (cured meats), fresh vegetables, fruit, and exquisite treats such as freshly made ricotta or a slice of *crostata*—a tart with homemade jam peeking out from lightly browned pastry. The wines produced at Titignano flow freely at dinner, bringing even the most bashful international traveler into the inevitably lively, multi-lingual recounting of notable sights, daily expeditions, and stories from home countries.

VIEWS OF TITIGNANO *(below) The village's castle on the left, farm buildings, church, and farmhouses enclose the stone courtyard. (opposite) The castle, seen from the rear.*

CASTELLO DI MONTALERA

The name Montalera, derived from *monte,* mountain, and Hera, the wife of Zeus, is apropos to the location of this 1530 structure, built around an existing medieval tower by military architect Antonio da Sangallo the Younger. From the lofty woods of the estate's mountaintop, a pristine plain silently unfolds to the shores of Lake Trasimeno, belying its tumultuous history.

It is here, on Lake Trasimeno's surrounding plain, where Hannibal defeated thousands of Romans during the Second Punic War. Virtually since the founding of Carthage (814 B.C.) and the subsequent founding of Rome (753 B.C.), conflict and distrust had raged between the two ancient powers. There were treaties and skirmishes, and then the Punic Wars. The Second Punic War followed Hannibal's legendary march over the French Alps with his Carthaginian elephants. Hannibal had planned an extraordinary surprise attack on Rome, intent on defeating the Empire. After his treacherous journey over the snow-covered mountains, he made his way toward Rome, following an eastern path along the northern shores of Lake Trasimeno. It was here, in June of 217 B.C., that Hannibal invoked the vengeance of Hera on fifteen thousand Roman troops and set the tone of battle for the coming months. More than two thousand years later, Lake Trasimeno and its surrounding plain are quietly serene, with only a hint of historical menace in the waters' changing colors, a reflection of winter's stormy skies.

VIEWS OF MONTALERA
(opposite) Detail of a kitchen in one of the estate's houses.
PAGES 126–127 *The plain surrounding Lake Trasimeno, viewed from the castle of Montalera. This freshwater lake is the largest body of water in landlocked Umbria.*

AZIENDA AGRICOLA LA MALVARINA

On a slope of Mount Subasio, between Assisi and Spello in Eastern Umbria, is Maria Maurillo's farm. Although visitors can lodge at Malvarina for a completely "self-catered" visit—to tour the nearby Umbrian towns and eat at restaurants every evening—to do so would be to miss the special, intimate quality of this estate. Maria Maurillo exudes warm hospitality, and she and her son Claudio and his family treat guests as they would old friends; lodging them in guest houses, providing them with homemade meals, and engaging them in convivial conversation. Maria, as well as cooking daily meals for visitors, conducts cooking lessons, emphasizing fresh Umbrian products and traditional country meals. Claudio is an enthusiastic

VIEWS OF MALVARINA

(below) Detail of antiques on the fireplace mantle in the sunny common breakfast room. (opposite) Claudio Fabrizi and his son, Filippo, both avid equestrians, with two of the estate's many horses.

horseman and gives guided horseback treks through the area's scenic countryside of forests, mountain slopes, and black-truffle fields.

After a day exploring Deruta's famous *majolica* pottery shops or paying tribute to St. Francis at Assisi, guests return to the *en famille* dining room, ready to dig into Maria's freshly prepared dinners. A typical meal includes an antipasto (appetizer); fresh pasta served with a traditional, meatless sauce; a meat dish; vegetables; and Maria's special sweets—all accompanied by wine and olive oil produced at Malvarina. A small shop below the dining room sells Malvarina's olive oil, fresh jams and preserves, lentils, and black truffles as well as the southern Italian, lemon liqueur called *limoncello.* This working farm is a wonderful example of a bed-and-breakfast style of accommodation, where visitors who delight in the comfort of fresh and flavorful country food and the warmth of a family environment might find a welcoming second home.

VIEWS OF MALVARINA

(opposite) A tower of pomegranates accentuates Maria's delicious homemade desserts. (below) The family's home, in shades of crimson and green, prepares for the holiday season.

IL CASTELLO DI GIOMICI

VIEWS OF GIOMICI

(opposite) Detail of an exterior wall of the castle's complex. (right) The living room of an apartment within the castle. The arched window demonstrates the width of the castle walls. PAGES 134–135 *The castle, its fortified parapets silhouetted against Umbria's autumn sky, guards the entrance to the 400-acre estate.*

Stone walls more than one meter thick silently testify to the endurance of this medieval castle and hamlet in north-central Umbria despite the innumerable wars and skirmishes it has witnessed. Indeed, the redoubt has stood since the end of the first millennium, and its conquest was first documented one hundred years later. Giomici's castellated towers guard the entrance to the 400-acre estate of woods and pastures, dotted with the area's characteristic ghostly white Chianina cattle.

Nestled within the green triangle of Gubbio, Assisi, and Perugia, the Vagni family castle sits beneath a blanket of country stillness. The tranquil existence of the farm revolves around grazing horses and autumn grape and olive harvests. Aptly enough, the *Senterio della Pace,* or Path of Peace, brushes the edge of the estate, winding its way from Assisi to Gubbio.

TELEPHONING OR FAXING ITALY Within the United States, dial 011 (signifying an international call), 39 (Italy's country code), the city code (the next 2–4 digits) and the number. Italy is in the process of adding a "0" in front of the city code, so we have included the "0" in the city code in our contact information.

From Italy, there is no need to dial the first two sets of numbers (011-39). You may begin the call with the city code (including the zero prior to the number).

CHOOSING AN ESTATE We recommend that as a first step you contact estates that interest you for additional information. Give the proprietor a general idea of when you would like to visit (such as "two weeks in June"), and ask them to send a brochure. Many have fax machines and e-mail addresses for a quicker response.

After receiving the basic information, consider in detail those things that you will require to make a stay in the countryside pleasurable for you and your companions. Careful planning will increase the likelihood of your satisfaction. During high season, vacancies are rare in the countryside, and if you are dissatisfied, procuring another post on short notice may be difficult.

COVERING THE BASICS When making your first inquires, keep in mind these basic questions:

__Does the estate take credit cards? Do they require a deposit?
__What is the minimum length of stay?
__Does the estate have specific arrival and departure days and times?
__What is the maximum number of people allowed in the accommodations?
__Are children and/or pets allowed?
__Is English spoken?

GAUGING THE LEVEL OF ACCOMMODATIONS As accommodations can vary from basic to luxurious, you may want to check the following:

__What is the ratio of bathrooms to bedrooms?
__Are kitchen appliances and/or washing machines provided?
__Will you have access to a private or shared pool?
__Does the estate offer any noteworthy recreations?

SERVICES Most houses are self-catering, meaning that guests are responsible for their own cooking, cleaning, and laundry. Almost every estate will provide services, charging according to extent of use, and some will arrange just about anything you can dream up. Ask in advance about the availability and cost of those services and extras that you will require, such as:

__Air conditioning and heating; use of fireplaces
__Television; telephones (including cellular); facsimile service; computer hook-ups
__Maid service; linens; baby cribs
__Food shopping and meal preparation
__Tour guides; cooking courses; wine and olive oil tastings
__Bicycle riding; horseback riding; tennis; hunting and fishing

ACCESSIBILITY These are not modern hotels, and many Italian buildings do not meet the United States' strict standards for wheelchair access. Be sure to ask in detail what provisions there are if you need unimpeded access.

IN THE AREA You may want to ask about the proximity of the following: churches with services; marked walking paths; private yards or gardens; special events; spas; museums; restaurants; shops and public beaches.

SEASONAL CONSIDERATIONS Italy, like many other European countries, can seem shut down in August, when Italians take their own vacations. Check if there are shops, restaurants, and museums nearby that remain open at the time of your stay. Besides national holidays, different regions have Saints' Days and festivals that may offer unexpected festivities or drawn shutters; be sure to inquire about when such events occur in the area you are considering.

TRANSPORTATION As the estates in this book are not located in cities, and thus not easily accessible by public transportation, we strongly suggest renting a car. An international driver's license may not be required, but check ahead with a local automotive club. Domestic car insurance policies on the whole do not transfer to foreign countries, so check thoroughly with your agent and then review in detail the coverage offered by the car rental agency. Remember that when flying directly from the United States, arrival in Italy is usually the day after departure. Consider that drivers will need some sleep on the plane, or think about staying locally for a day or so to rest and recover from jet lag before setting out on the road.

RENTAL PRICING Most of these rental houses and apartments are significantly less expensive than Italy's hotels. The basic price usually does not include extras, such as those things that are indicated in the "services" section. For a general guideline, we have established three categories, based on the price for two people, whether sharing a larger accommodation or staying in a one bedroom apartment and are indicated by the **$** symbol. The prices are per week and range from low to high season. These prices are based on an exchange rate in January, 1999. High season usually includes the months of May through September and the Christmas holiday, but varies at each estate. [**$**] From $225 to 350 in low season to $700 in high season [**$$**] From $350 to $700 in low season to $1,400 in high season[**$$$**] more than $700 per week to more than $1,400 in high season Those that include some meals in their basic pricing are indicated with an ⊗.

AZIENDA AGRICOLA COLOGNOLE

The owners of Colognole have created an atmosphere that reflects this woodsy, wild estate situated on the road up to Montegiovi. The apartments within the houses are simply furnished (though each house has its own pool) and have views to the well-tended estate. **$**

CONTACT
Azienda Agricola Colognole
Via del Palagio, 15
50068 Colognole Rufina (FI)

 011-39-055-8319870  011-39-055-8319605

TENUTA DI BOSSI

The Bossi estate rents houses, varying from a small villa to *poderi,* or farmhouses, with decor ranging accordingly. The houses are situated around the olive groves and vineyards of the estate and each has its own garden and parking. **$**

CONTACT
Tenuta di Bossi
Via dello Stracchino, 32
50065, Pontessieve (FI)

 011-39-055-8317830  011-39-055-8364008

CASTELLO IL TREBBIO

The owner of the Trebbio castle strives to preserve the rustic character of the houses surrounding the castle by furnishing them in a simple, country style. Visits to this Medici castle's courtyard, garden, and magnificent pergola can be arranged by appointment. **$**

CONTACT
Castello del Trebbio
50037 San Piero a Sieve (FI)

 011-39-055-848088  011-39-055-8498470

For information about the castle and for visits to the castle's garden, call *Associazione Turismo e Ambiente* at 011-39-055-8458793.

FATTORIA DI MAIANO

Fattoria di Maiano offers apartments in its formerly cloistered convent, farm buildings, and country houses. All of the accommodations have a blend of antique and modern furnishings and share views of both the city of Florence and the surrounding countryside. **$$**

CONTACT

Fattoria di Maiano
Via Benedetto da Maiano 11
Fiesole (FI)

✆ 011-39-055-599600 or 597089

FAX 011-39-055-599640

TENUTA DI CAPEZZANA

The Capezzana estate's apartments, which are within the main villa, are rented independently or as a component of its cooking courses. The five-day food programs include shopping, preparing foods, wine tastings, and transportation to and from Florence. **$$**

CONTACT

Tenuta di Capezzana
Via Capezzana, 100
59011 Localita Seano
Carmignano (PO)

✆ 011-39-055-8706005 or 8706091

FAX 011-39-055-8706673

UNITED STATES AGENT FOR CAPEZZANA:
Marlene Levinson,
55 Raycliff Terrace, San Francisco, CA, 94115
✆ 415/928-7711 FAX 415/928-7789

website: www.capezzana.it
e-mail: capezzana@dada.it

FATTORIA LE CORTI

The large apartments at Le Corti are well furnished; decorating details are simple and stylish. Each apartment has its own fenced yard (Italians refer to them as "gardens"), fireplace, and all modern conveniences. This estate has joined with other partners to form a booking service for its apartments. **$$**

CONTACT

Agritourism Manager
Via S. Piero di Sotto, 5
50026 San Casciano Val di Pesa (FI)

✆ 011-39-055-829-0105

FAX 011-39-055-8290106 or 011-39-055-8290089

e-mail: stagchianti@ftbcc.it

CASTELLO DI BROLIO

The Brolio estate offers apartments both within the castle and in a nearby *podere* (farmhouse). The castle apartments are grand in scale and furnished with the personal belongings of the Ricasoli family and are therefore more expensive than those in surrounding buildings The *podere* apartments are decorated well and have small gardens. This estate has joined with other partners to form a booking service for its apartments. **$$**

CONTACT

Agritourism Manager
Via S. Piero di Sotto, 5
50026 San Casciano Val di Pesa (FI)

✆ 011-39-055-829-0105

FAX 011-39-055-8290106 or 011-39-055-8290089

e-mail: stagchianti@ftbcc.it

CASTELLO DI CACCHIANO

The distinctive accommodations offered by the Castello di Cacchiano are within the tiny hamlet adjacent to the wine cellars of the estate. The furnishings are tasteful; the apartments charming. This estate has joined with other partners to form a booking service for its apartments. **$$**

CONTACT

Agritourism Manager
Via S. Piero di Sotto, 5
50026 San Casciano Val di Pesa (FI)

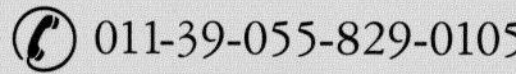

011-39-055-829-0105

FAX 011-39-055-8290106 or 011-39-055-8290089

e-mail stagchianti@ftbcc.it

FATTORIA CASTELLO DI BIBBIONE

The owners here have created a true balance between modern renovation and antique furnishings, resulting in very stylish accommodations in stone houses dotting the estate. The attention to decorating detail is notable; the family uses its own belongings to furnish the apartments. **$$**

CONTACT

Ginevra Jatta
Via Collina, 66
50020 Montefiridolfi (FI)

011-39-335-8106514

with FAX 011-39-055/8249231

CASTELLO DI FONTERUTOLI

The apartments of the Fonterutoli hamlet evoke the feeling of a private family environment. All are tastefully furnished and share the hamlet with a restaurant/bar and the offices of the family's well-known wine business. This estate has joined with other partners to form a booking service for its apartments. **$$**

CONTACT

Agritourism Manager
Via S. Piero di Sotto, 5
50026 San Casciano Val di Pesa (FI)

011-39-055-829-0105

FAX 011-39-055-8290106 or 011-39-055-8290089

e-mail: stagchianti@ftbcc.it

CASTELLO DI VOLPAIA

The charming hamlet of Volpaia offers thoughtfully furnished apartments in this formerly fortified village. It is a bustling town, comprised of local inhabitants, a popular restaurant/bar, wine cellars, and *frantoio* (olive oil mill). **$$**

CONTACT

Fattoria Castello di Volpaia di Giovannella Stianti
Volpaia, 1
53017 Radda in Chianti (SI)

011-39-577-738066

FAX 011-39-577-738619

TENUTA DI PETROLO

The houses and large villa of the Petrolo estate are artistically and comfortably furnished; each has its own pool. This large estate offers seclusion and privacy among olive groves and vineyards. The 11th-century *pieve* (parish church) can be visited upon request. **$**

CONTACT

Lucia Sanjust Bazzocchi
Localita Galatrona
52020 Mercatale
Valdarno (AR)

011-39-055-9911322 FAX 011-39-055-992749

CASTELLO DI POGGIO PETROIO

The estate of Poggio Petroio offers six cozy, elaborately detailed apartments decorated by the owner, a former interior designer. The apartments line the entrance to the courtyard near the medieval tower and dog museum. Entrance to the museum is by appointment. **$$$**

CONTACT

Achille Alessandro Conti
Castello di Poggio Petroio
50028 Tavarnelle V.P. (FI)

✆ 011-39-055-8070004 or 8070103

FAX 011-39-055-807-0004

VILLA VISTARENNI

The apartments offered by Villa Vistarenni are within the villa and in a large *podere* a short distance from the courtyard. The furnishings are a combination of antique and Tuscan, and all guests share use of a pool and tennis court. This estate has joined with other partners to form a booking service for its apartments. **$$**

CONTACT

Agritourism Manager
Via S. Piero di Sotto, 5
50026 San Casciano Val di Pesa (FI)

✆ 011-39-055-829-0105

FAX 011-39-055-8290106 or 011-39-055-8290089

e-mail: stagchianti@ftbcc.it

CASTELLO DI MONTALTO

The houses and apartments of Castello di Montalto are thoughtfully furnished and all but one has its own fireplace. There are two tower apartments; one is an elegant, large accommodation with piano, and the other is an intimate space for two. **$$**

CONTACT

Agriturismo al Castello di Montalto
53019 Castelnuovo Berardenga (SI)

✆ 011-39-577-355675 FAX 011-39-577-355682

website: www.montalto.it
email: montalto@iol.it

IL CASTELLO DI RIPA D'ORCIA

The apartments and bed and breakfast rooms offered at the Castle of Ripa d'Orcia are situated within the fortified walls, in the buildings surrounding the castle. The rooms are simple and spacious; the restaurant serves breakfast and dinner. **$$**

CONTACT

Castello di Ripa d'Orcia
Val d'Orcia
53023 Castiglione d'Orcia (SI)

✆ 011-39-577-897317 or 897376

FAX 011-39-577-898038

website: www.nautilus-mp.com/ripa

LA FOCE

The apartments on the large property of La Foce are beautifully furnished. The estate's castle, Castelluccio, is the site of art and music festivals and other events. Of special interest is La Foce's garden, designed by English architect Cecil Pinsent; tours are available and it is open to the public once a week. **$$**

CONTACT

La Foce
63, Strada della Vittoria
53042 Chianciano Terme (SI)

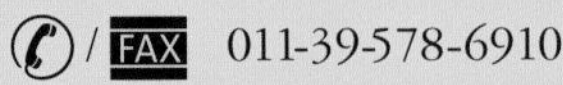
✆ / FAX 011-39-578-69101

LUCIGNANELLO BANDINI

The three apartments off of the piazza in the tiny hamlet of Lucignano d'Asso are all designed to accommodate four persons, but will hold six. Each has been cheerily restored with comfortable furniture and frescoed walls. **$$$**

CONTACT

Lucignanello Bandini
S. Giovanni d'Asso (SI)

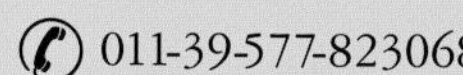 011-39-577-823068 FAX 011-39-577-823082

FATTORIA DI COSONA

The Cosona Villa offers apartments in *poderi* that surround the main house. The apartments are simple, rustic, and fully self-catering. **$**

CONTACT

Maria Bichi Ruspoli Forteguerri
Fattoria di Cosona
Localita Cosona
53026 Pienza (SI)

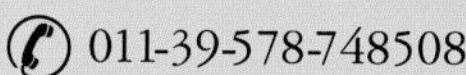 011-39-578-748508

CASTELLO ROMITORIO

The apartments offered by Castello Romitorio are situated in a very carefully renovated house on the estate and in an ancient water mill. The kitchens are lavishly modern and the other rooms are comfortably furnished. **$$$**

CONTACT

Mr. Carlo Vittori
Via dei Canneti 37/B
53027 S. Quirico d'Orcia, (SI)

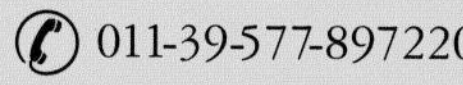 011-39-577-897220

FAX 011-39-577-897026

e-mail: cavittor@tim.it

VILLA OLIVA-BUONVISI

Villa Oliva-Buonvisi offers tastefully decorated apartments in buildings surrounding the villa. Rental includes use of the beautiful swimming pool, tennis court (made of artificial grass, which is a surface between clay and grass), and extensive gardens. **$$**

CONTACT

Solemar, a booking agency in Florence at 011-39-055-239361.

PERALTA

Peralta's altitude of nearly 1,000 feet above sea level provides beautiful vistas of the Mediterranean Sea and the Island of Corsica. The apartments are artistically furnished and quite comfortable. There is a bar for all guests and a restaurant for bed and breakfast accommodations. Access to the Peralta hamlet is via a narrow, switchback road through the woods and the hamlet itself is comprised of buildings with steep steps between. Peralta indicates that it is unsuitable for children under five years of age. **$**

CONTACT

Peralta
Camaiore, 55041 (LU)

 011-39-584-951-230

VILLA DEL MONTE

The apartments of Villa del Monte are within the villa; all share use of the roomy gardens, pool, and grounds. The accommodations range in size from the tower apartment, a romantic loft space for two, to a large, sprawling apartment in the villa. **$$**

Open April to November

CONTACT

Villa del Monte
Via Canonica, 6
53037 San Gimignano (SI)

011-39-577-944925

 011-39-577-944811

FATTORIA DI MONTELOPIO

The Montelopio estate offers two types of accommodations: a large apartment in the main villa and smaller apartments in a restructured house within the abundant garden. The Villa apartment is decorated with antique possessions and photographs, while the independent house has a very contemporary feel. All have modern conveniences. **$**

CONTACT
Eredi Mazzetti
Fattoria di Montelopio
Fraz. Fabbrica Peccioli (PI)
Avv. Leopoldo Mazzetti
011-39-06-688-03543 FAX 011/39-06-688-05144

e-mail: gmdapers@tin.it

FATTORIA DI MONTEGEMOLI

The beautifully restructured apartments of Montegemoli are large, airy, and have magnificent views. They are decorated in a modern, stylish fashion and have all of the modern conveniences. **$**

CONTACT
Maria Pia and Teresa d'Albertis
Fattoria di Montegemoli
Pomaranche (PI)
Avv. Leopoldo Mazzetti
011-39-06-688-03543 FAX 011-39-06-688-05144

e-mail: gmdapers@tin.it

CASTELLO DI PETROIA

Castello di Petroia offers hotel-type accommodations within the castle, complete with breakfast, mini-bars and services. The host is welcoming and meals are eaten together in his magnificent drawing and dining rooms. **$$$**

CONTACT
Castello di Petroia
Localita Petroia
06020 Scritto di Gubbio (PG)
011-39-75-920287 or 920109
FAX 011-39-75-920108

website: www.infoservice.it
e-mail: castello.petroia@infoservice.it

FATTORIA DI TITIGNANO

Guests may stay within Titignano's castle in nicely furnished bedrooms with en suite bathrooms. Across the *piazzale* (small courtyard, or piazza), the village's former houses have been converted into suites, some with just enough kitchen to make coffee or help with a baby. These apartments are furnished in a modern style and offer heating for fall and winter stays. **$$**

CONTACT
Fattoria di Titignano
Localita Titignano-Orvieto (Terni) 06010
011-39-763-308000 or 011-39-763-308022
FAX 011-39-763-308002

e-mail: fattoria@orvienet.it

CASTELLO DI MONTALERA

The houses available for rent at Montalera have been painstakingly restored by the owners. These houses are truly independent and have views of Lake Trasimeno. **$$**

CONTACT
Solemar, a booking agency in Florence at 011-39-055-239361.

AZIENDA AGRICOLA LA MALVARINA

The Malvarina estate offers apartments that are situated around the home of the extremely hospitable Maria Maurillo, her son Claudio Fabrizi, and his family. These lodgings offer an intimate, family-oriented environment marked by simple furnishings and very fine food prepared by Maria Maurillo. **$$**

CONTACT

Agriturismo Malvarina
Localita Malvarina
Capodacqua di Assisi, Assisi (PG)

  011-39-75-806-4280

website: www.umbria.net/malvarina
e-mail: malvarina@umbria.net

ORGANIZED TOURS, TASTINGS AND COOKING LESSONS:
Gabriele Dellanave, with headquarters in Minnesota, USA toll-free telephone 888-287-8733.

 507-287-9890

e-mail: gabriele@hps.com

IL CASTELLO DI GIOMICI

The apartments offered by the Giomici Castle are located either inside the castle, in buildings across the piazza of the castle, or in surrounding farmhouses. They are simply decorated and provide for every need. **$**

CONTACT

Agriturismo Il Castello di Giomici
06029 Valfabbrica (PG)

011-39-75-901243

FAX 011-39-75-901713

website: www.IlCastelloDiGiomici.it
e-mail: Reception@IlCastelloDiGiomici.it

PAGE 144 *Detail of vine-covered house at the La Foce estate.*

ACKNOWLEDGMENTS

This book comes to fruition with the help of a diverse group of generous people. Beyond the typically warm and welcoming Tuscan and Umbrian homeowners, many of the proprietors included in the book greeted us like family, generously bestowing upon us inordinate amounts of their time and patient attention. We deeply thank all of our hosts and wish them continued good fortune. Early enthusiasts who significantly contributed to the book include James Waller, Jay Anning, Marisa Bulzone, Ensley Eikenburg, Karen Cure, Tony Verga, and Tannaz. Anna Cataldi, Joyce Petschek, Maria Teresa Train, Joanie Shoemaker, and Jo-Lynne Worley provided wisdom and guidance. Amelia Costigan, gifted designer, and Abigail Wilentz, diligent editor, proved tireless and endlessly supportive. Charles Miers, thank you for the opportunity. Finally, thanks to good friends Giovanni Marchi, George Romanation, and Bill Arnold who gave special support, and to Tom Murphy, Thomas Laage, and Mark Carpenter without whom the writing of this book could never have happened.